TURNING INWARD

Also by Cheryl Richardson

Books

Stand Up for Your Life:
Develop the Courage, Confidence, and Character to Fulfill Your Greatest Potential

Life Makeovers:
52 Practical and Inspiring Ways to Improve Your Life One Week at a Time

Take Time for Your Life:
A Personal Coach's Seven-Step Program for Creating the Life You Want

Audio Programs

Finding Your Passion (4-tape program or 4-CD program)

Tuning In: Listening to the Voice of Your Soul (CD)

Card Deck

Self-Care Cards (a 52-card deck)

Please visit the Hay House Website at: hayhouse.com

TURNING INWARD

A Private Journal for Self-Reflection

Cheryl Richardson

Hay House, Inc.
Carlsbad, California • Sydney, Australia
Canada • Hong Kong • United Kingdom

Published and distributed in the United States by:
   Hay House, Inc., P.O. Box 5100, Carlsbad, CA 92018-5100 • (800) 654-5126 • (800) 650-5115 (fax)
www.hayhouse.com
   Hay House Australia Pty Ltd, P.O. Box 515, Brighton-Le-Sands, NSW 2216 • *phone:* 1800 023 516
e-mail: info@hayhouse.com.au

Editorial supervision: Jill Kramer • *Design:* Christy Salinas

ISBN 1-4019-0114-X

05 04 03 02   4 3 2 1
1st printing, August 2002

Printed in the United States of America

Dear Friend,

Developing a solid relationship with yourself is the key to living a life of meaning and purpose. There's nothing more important than this intimate connection. As you create a strong attachment to your inner life, you're better able to make choices that reflect your deepest longings and desires. One of the best ways to build a strong bond with yourself is by journaling. For more than 25 years, I've kept a journal—a private place to record my thoughts, feelings, and reactions to life experiences. This personal practice has taught me to turn to and rely on my own innate wisdom. Now, I'd like to support you in doing the same.

I've designed this journal to help you begin a process of self-reflection. The goal is simple: to get to know yourself better. To make this practice easier, I offer you questions to answer and sentences to finish, with the goal of completing two pages for each one. Like the mind that feels scattered during the beginning stages of meditation, the first page of journaling may feel more lilke reporting than connecting with a wise part of yourself. If you keep at it, you'll soon find that your mind and heart come into alignment and you begin to write from a deeper, more feeling-oriented place. Writing from this place will connect you with the voice of your soul.

There's no perfect way to journal. Just ponder each question or sentence and write whatever comes to mind. Don't worry about spelling, grammar, or writing every day. What matters most is that you get started and stay with it. It takes time and discipline to buld a new, self-honoring habit.

Make sure that you keep your journal tucked away in a secure place so you have the privacy you need to be honest with yourself. Telling the truth about your life is the first step toward positive change. So close your eyes, take a few relaxing deep breaths, and start writing. Enjoy!

— Cheryl

WHAT'S

great

about

your life?

WHAT are the

top five most

important

priorities in your

life right now?

Why are they

important to you,

and what do you

need to do to

honor them?

WHAT have been

the highlights of

your life so far?

The lowlights?

What have you

learned from each

experience?

WHAT are you

feeling right now?

Keep writing until

you shift from

thinking to feeling.

WHAT do your

home and work

environments say

about you?

WHAT gets

you excited?

What makes you

feel highly

motivated and

enthusiastic?

WHAT

I'm really

afraid of is . . .

IF I had all the

courage and

support I needed,

I would . . .

TODAY, choose a

favorite quote and

copy it here.

Then write

about what

it means to you.

FIND a photo of

yourself as a child.

Think back to when

you were that age.

What did you

dream about or

hope for?

RECALL a

favorite memory

and write about it.

What makes this

memory so special?

THINK about a

person who has

influenced your life

in a powerful way.

Next, write about

how this person has

shaped your thinking,

your beliefs, and

your actions.

IF you had all the

time in the world,

what ten things

would you most

want to do?

Describe them

in detail.

THINK of a time

when you were

exceptionally

courageous and

emotionally strong.

What strengths did

you call upon?

How has this

experience

influenced your

life today?

WHAT was the

attitude in your

family toward

money?

How have these

messages affected

you as an adult?

START an

abundance list here.

Learn to see the

blessings you

receive each day by

returning to this

page often to

add to the list.

WHEN did you

first experience

falling in love?

What was it like?

How have your

views on love

changed over

the years?

What does love

mean to you now?

CHOOSE one
path or desire from
your earlier years
that you
didn't pursue.
Then, imagine that
you *did* take that
road, and write
about how your life
would have been
different from this
perspective.

IF you had all the

money, time,

confidence, and

self-awareness in

the world, how

would your life

change?

IDENTIFY one
person whom
you admire.
What
characteristics
make this person
admirable?
Are these qualities
that you need
to develop?
If so, pick one, and
create a plan that
will allow you to
cultivate this trait.

WRITE a letter to

God, the Divine, a

Higher Power, the

Universe, or Spirit.

If you could meet

this Presence

face-to-face, what

would you most

want to say?

MAKE a list

of your favorite

books, magazines,

and catalogs.

If these items could

speak, what would

they say about you?

What do they have

in common?

44

THE healthy and

not-so-healthy

ways in which I

comfort myself

when I'm upset,

tired, or

overwhelmed are . . .

IF your life

were a movie,

what would the

overall message be?

Write the

storyline here.

WHO or what

drains your energy?

What do you need

to do about it?

IF you were to take

exceptional care of

your financial

health, what five

things would you

do differently

and why?

HOW has your

spiritual upbringing

affected your

relationship with a

power greater than

yourself?

WHAT qualities

do you most love

and admire

about yourself?

Why?

How have these

qualities served you

and others?

IMAGINE your

perfect vacation.

Where would you go?

Who would you

take with you?

What would you do

(or not do)?

WHAT three

boundaries do you

need to set in order

to create the space

for more success

in your life?

IF you decided to

use your talents

and gifts in an even

greater way, what

would you do

differently?

WHAT do you

stand for, feel

passionate about,

or deeply

believe in?

IF you had a

chance to trade

places with one

person (alive or

dead) for a day,

who would it be?

Why?

WRITE

your own

prayer.

IMAGINE that you're qualified to do any job in the world. What ten jobs would you most like to try? Why?

IF you could alter

or relive one

incident in your

life, which one

would it be?

What would you do

differently?

How do you think

your life would

change?

IMAGINE yourself as the opposite of who you are (introvert vs. extrovert, or disorganized vs. organized) and write about how you'd behave differently at work, in your relationships, or while having fun over the course of a week.

LIST 15 skills

that you possess.

Then, review this

list and circle the

ones you love

to use most.

How is this

information

reflected in your

daily life?

WHAT do

you want?

What do

you need?

WHAT blessings

would you like to

receive right now?

How might they

serve you?

DREAMS are the

doorway to the soul.

Write about a

recent dream you

had, even if you

only remember

part of it.

WHO are you

jealous or envious

of, and why?

What is this person

doing that you

need to be doing?

WHEN you look

back over your

romantic

relationships, what

patterns or themes

can you identify?

IF you could wave

a magic wand and

change one area of

your life, which one

would it be?

Explain.

CHOOSE several

favorite songs from

your school days

and write about the

thoughts and

feelings they evoke

as you listen

to them.

CUT out five

images from a

favorite magazine

or catalog and paste

them here.

Why are you drawn

to these images?

What might your

soul be trying

to tell you?

HOW do you care

for your spiritual

well-being?

GO through your

favorite keepsakes.

Choose five special

items and write

about why they're

important to you.

WHO are the

important people

in your life?

What do you love

most about them?

DESCRIBE your

personal style.

What is the mood

or tone that your

image projects?

HOW have you

grown over the

last year?

What qualities have

you developed?

How have you

strengthened your

character?

What challenges

did you successfully

overcome?

DESCRIBE your

path of spiritual

development up

to this point

in your life.

WHAT do

you value

most in life?

IF someone were

to ask, "Who are

you?" how would

you respond?

HOW do you

need to improve

your health?

If you

accomplished this

goal, how would

your life change?

INTERVIEW

three close friends

or family members

and ask them to

describe the

qualities that make

you unique

and special.

Write down their

thoughts here.

IMAGINE that

you could spend an

entire day being a

child again, without

any responsibilities

or worries.

What would you do?

WHAT legacy do

you wish to leave

for others?

WHAT do you

dream about doing

in your life?

What's

stopping you?

HOW has your life

shifted as a result

of completing this

journal?

How has your

relationship with

yourself changed?

About the Author

*Bestselling author and lecturer **Cheryl Richardson** supports busy people in achieving success without compromising their quality of life. Her work has been covered widely in the media, including **Oprah**, the **Today** show, **Good Morning America**, the **New York Times**, **Good Housekeeping**, and **Publisher's Weekly**. To subscribe to Cheryl's free weekly on-line newsletter, visit her Website at: **cherylrichardson.com**.*

Other Hay House Titles of Related Interest

Dream Journal,
by Leon Nacson

A Garden of Thoughts,
by Louise L. Hay

Hay House Blank Journals:
All Is Well in My World
Insights
Power Thoughts

A Journal of Love and Healing: Transcending Grief,
by Sylvia Browne and Nancy Dufresne

The Love and Power Journal,
by Lynn V. Andrews

Love Yourself, Heal Your Life Workbook,
by Louise L. Hay

You Can Heal Your Life Companion Book,
by Louise L. Hay

All of the above are available at your local bookstore,
or may be ordered through Hay House, Inc.:

(800) 654-5126 or (760) 431-7695
(800) 650-5115 (fax) or (760) 431-6948 (fax)
www.hayhouse.com

We hope you enjoyed this Hay House book.
If you would like to receive a free catalog featuring additional
Hay House books and products, or if you would like information
about the Hay Foundation, please contact:

Hay House, Inc.
P.O. Box 5100
Carlsbad, CA 92018-5100

(760) 431-7695 or (800) 654-5126
(760) 431-6948 (fax) or (800) 650-5115 (fax)
www.hayhouse.com

Hay House Australia Pty Ltd
P.O. Box 515
Brighton-Le-Sands, NSW 2216
phone: 1800 023 516
e-mail: info@hayhouse.com.au